Holidays

Easter

by Rebecca Pettiford

Bullfrog Books

Ideas for Parents and Teachers

Bullfrog Books let children practice reading informational text at the earliest reading levels. Repetition, familiar words, and photo labels support early readers.

Before Reading

- Discuss the cover photo. What does it tell them?
- Look at the picture glossary together. Read and discuss the words.

Read the Book

- "Walk" through the book and look at the photos. Let the child ask questions. Point out the photo labels.
- Read the book to the child, or have him or her read independently.

After Reading

- Prompt the child to think more. Ask: Does your family celebrate Easter? What sorts of things do you see when people celebrate Easter? Why is spring a good time for Easter?

Bullfrog Books are published by Jump!
5357 Penn Avenue South
Minneapolis, MN 55419
www.jumplibrary.com

Library of Congress Cataloging-in-Publication Data
Pettiford, Rebecca.
 Easter / by Rebecca Pettiford.
    pages cm.—(Holidays)
 Includes bibliographical references and index.
 Summary: "This photo-illustrated book for early readers describes the Christian holiday of Easter and the things people do to celebrate"
Provided by publisher.
 ISBN 978-1-62031-129-5 (hardcover)
 ISBN 978-1-62496-196-0 (ebook)
 1. Easter—Juvenile literature. I. Title.
 BV55.P43 2014
 263'.93—dc23
                                        2013049157

Editor: Wendy Dieker
Series Designer: Ellen Huber
Book Designer: Lindaanne Donohoe
Photo Researcher: Kurtis Kinneman

Photo Credits: All photos by Shutterstock except: iStock, 5, 8–9, 8 (inset); Ariel Skelley/Blend Images/Corbis, 14–15; Jose Luis Pelaez Inc/Blend Images/Corbis, 12–13; Ocean/Corbis, 20–21

Printed in the United States of America at Corporate Graphics in North Mankato, Minnesota.
3-2014
10 9 8 7 6 5 4 3 2 1

Table of Contents

What Is Easter?

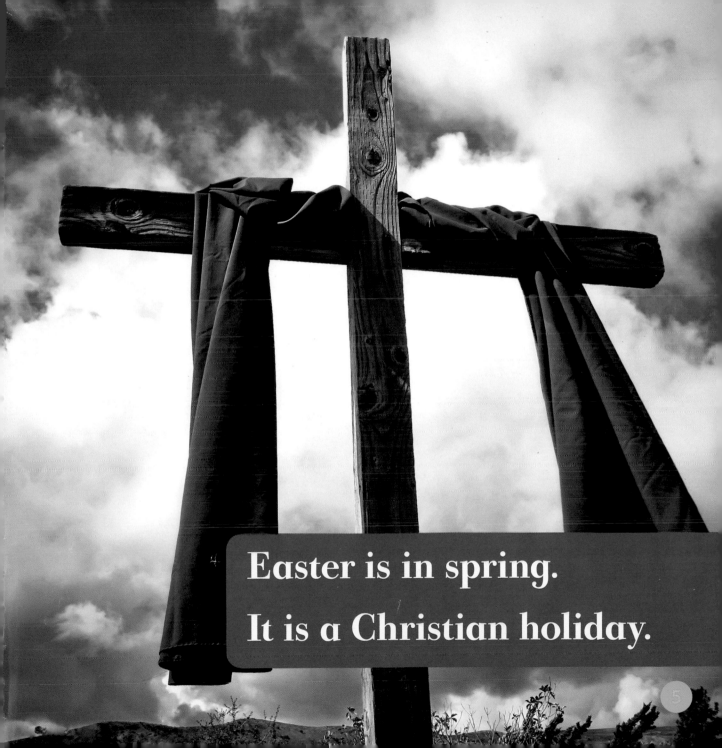

Easter is in spring.
It is a Christian holiday.

What do Christians believe?

Jesus was God's son.

He died on a cross.

In three days, he came back to life.

It is Easter Sunday.

We go to church.

We learn about
Jesus' new life.

On Easter, we celebrate new life.
A new flower grows.

A chick hatches.

An egg is a symbol
of new life.

We dye eggs.

Jada's egg is green.

It is an Easter
egg hunt!

Eve finds an egg.

A baby animal
is new life.

Look!

It's a baby bunny.

Is it the Easter
bunny?

Ty gets a basket.
It has candy in it.

18

jelly beans

The jelly beans look like eggs.
See the bunny? It's chocolate!

Happy Easter!

Symbols of Easter

cross

Jesus

Easter bunny

Easter eggs

Picture Glossary

dye
To change the color of something by soaking it in colored liquid.

jelly beans
A candy shaped like a bean or egg with a soft center.

hatch
To break out of an egg.

symbol
An object that represents something else. Flowers are a symbol of life.

Index

To Learn More

Learning more is as easy as 1, 2, 3.

1) Go to www.factsurfer.com

2) Enter "Easter" into the search box.

3) Click the "Surf" button to see a list of websites.

With factsurfer.com, finding more information is just a click away.